MEL BAY'S
FINGER GYMNASTICS
WARM-UP, FLEXIBILITY, SPEED & STRENGTH STUDIES

by Charles Chapman

CD CONTENTS

Visit us on the Web at www.melbay.com — E-mail us at email@melbay.com

TABLE OF CONTENTS

INTRODUCTION

Finger gymnastics is a term used for warm-ups, stretching, and any type of practice exercise that develops technique and stamina while preventing music-related injuries. Everyone has a special warm-up regimen and many guitarists use the warm-up as a type of meditation that not only warms the muscles, but also places the mind in the proper perspective to create and perform at its best. The exercises in this book are time-tested and will keep your technique at its optimum while helping to insure injury-free performance. The entire text is not meant to be played daily. Pick and choose the exercises which you feel will be the most beneficial. The exception is chapter I which should become a part of your daily lifetime practice routine.

Most musicians will suffer from numerous music-related injuries during their career; 99.9% of these can be avoided. Just adhere to the few basic suggestions below.

I. Always practice in a consistent manner and try to slowly build up your stamina. Even though it is very difficult, practice for the same amount of time every day. Not touching your instrument for three days and then practicing for six hours is an invitation to injury. The great artists who practice ten hours a day have built up to it. It's like athletics; you don't start out running a marathon.

II. Never practice the same exercise for long periods of time. If you need to build technique in a certain area, alternate between three or four different types of exercises. Building up one set of muscles can cause an imbalance in your muscular/skeletal system which can lead to great discomfort.

III. Be careful when switching between instruments. If you play a solid body guitar with light string gauges and suddenly switch to an acoustic guitar with high action and much heavier strings, beware. Build up to playing your new instrument over a long period of time or problems will occur. Believe it or not, the same applies when going from a guitar with high action and heavy strings to a guitar with low action and light strings. Switching to a guitar with nylon strings or to an electric bass, mandolin, banjo or other instrument can cause problems as well, so proceed with caution. If you play these instruments frequently it is generally not a problem; only when you play these instruments on an occasional basis will this problem rear its ugly head.

IV. Use a good quality, wide, preferably leather strap—especially if you play a heavy instrument. It always amazes me how guitarists will spend a lot of money on an instrument only to hang it over their shoulder on something akin to a piece of rope. A good quality strap not only looks good, but can prevent problems down the road that are often misdiagnosed and can impede your musical development.

Besides warming up your muscles and limbering up your tendons, these basic exercises will improve your technique in both hands. You will become more accurate, increase the speed at which you can execute your lines, and develop better independence between your left and right hand.

Stay healthy, warm-up and stretch, or the rest of the world may never enjoy what you're capable of achieving.

HOW TO USE CD

On the enclosed CD you will find three versions of the exercises in chapters I and II. No matter how proficient your technique is do not attempt to execute the third example on your first practice session of the day—BUILD UP TO IT. If time permits, do the first two chapters three times a day, executing a different, more advanced version of the exercises each time. It should take no more than five or six minutes to go through these exercises.

In chapter III, bass and rhythm accompaniments are included for many of the examples. Matching the pitch and articulation with a rhythm background will not only assist in warming up, stretching, and building stamina, but will make your practice a more pleasurable experience.

NOTATION OF RIGHT AND LEFT HANDS

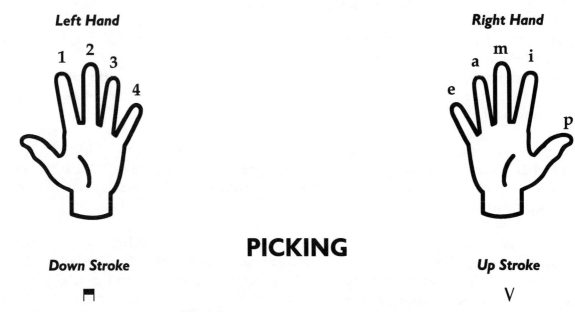

Left Hand

Right Hand

PICKING

Down Stroke

Up Stroke

V

ABOUT THE AUTHOR

Charles Chapman is a Professor in the Guitar Department at Berklee College of Music where he has taught since 1972. He is a versatile jazz guitarist with extensive performing and recording experience. Charles has appeared in the "pit bands" of such notable theater productions as Grease, Will Roger's Follies, Man of LaMancha, Annie, Finnian's Rainbow, Fiddler On The Roof, Mame and Anything Goes. He released *In Black and White*, a jazz duet album with bassist Rich Appleman in 1996, on DC Records. He has performed at the California NAMM Show and was a featured performer at the George Van Eps Tribute Concert during the 1999 Los Angeles Jazz Guitar Festival. Charles performs on a regular basis at guitar shows and jazz festivals internationally.

As a music copyist Charles has worked for such prestigious publishing houses as Mel Bay, Schirmer, Hal Leonard, Berklee Press and numerous music periodicals, as well as many prominent arrangers.

Charles is an artist endorser for Fender/Guild Corporation and Double Treble custom guitar straps.

Chapter I
WARM-UPS
Non-Instrument Warm-Ups

When you see an athlete stretching and doing breathing exercises no one seems to think it's a strange or a weird phenomenon, but let a musician try it and see how many heads turn. Playing guitar is a very physical endeavor and, as in sports, precautions should be taken to prevent debilitating injuries. As a guitar instructor for many years, I've seen hundreds of guitarist's careers impeded or ruined by music-related injuries such as strained muscles, tendinitis, carpal tunnel syndrome, or pinched nerves. Doing a few simple warm-ups before you even take the instrument out of the case can be very helpful. Most music-related physical problems can be eliminated by examining how you practice and play. You must first set up a comprehensive warm-up and stretching routine to fit your individual needs and schedule. Besides warming up your muscles and limbering up your tendons, they will improve your technique and accuracy in both hands.

I have found the following three exercises to be very helpful.

Wrist Rotations

1. While sitting or standing, hold your right elbow with your left hand; bend your right elbow so your hand is straight up, palm toward center.

2. Keeping your right elbow supported, rotate your right wrist to the left for five complete rotations.

3. In the same position rotate your right wrist to the right for five complete rotations.

Make five complete circles to one side, then five to the opposite side with one hand. Change hands and repeat procedure. Do one to three sets as warm-ups, no more. Never force or over stretch—just keep it relaxed with a gentle stretch.

Hand Stretches

1. Bend your elbows and raise your hands, with your fingers stretched wide open.

2. Slowly close your hands tightly and clench your fists.

Keep your stretch gentle and never strain or push. These can be done one hand at a time or both simultaneously.

Do one to three sets.

Finger Stretches

1. Bend your elbows with the palms of your hands facing downward as though you were playing a keyboard. Strike the notes with your little or fourth finger, keeping your other fingers raised.

2. Leaving your little fingers down, strike the next notes with both ring fingers.

3. Next, hit the notes with the middle fingers of both hands.

4. Now strike the notes with your index fingers.

5. Last, play the note firmly with both thumbs.

These warm-ups can be varied depending on your needs. Feel free to experiment and add repetitions and exercises. If any part of your body is stiff or sore, gently stretch that area as well before you pick up your guitar. All areas of the body are connected and if one is not functioning properly it will affect your performance.

Warm-Ups with Instrument
Across the Fingerboard

This warm-up is my absolute favorite and I cite this particular exercise as the reason I have been able to maintain my technique over the years, even when life has pulled me away from my guitar. If I have time for nothing else, I will do this exercise every day. In fact, I usually do it eight or nine times during the course of a 24-hour period. It involves very little concentration and works both hands to their optimum level. All fingers of the left hand get an equal amount of exercise (including the fourth finger which often is overlooked) and it gives your right hand an excellent workout as well. Use alternate picking on all the following exercises. If you play fingerstyle, feel free to use thumb and index finger or index finger and middle finger.

Place your fourth finger on the first string, twelfth fret and play chromatically descending to the ninth fret using each of the fingers of the left hand. Repeat this on each string, working across the fingerboard to the sixth string. When you get to the ninth fret, sixth string, slide your first finger back to the eighth fret and play chromatically, ascending to the eleventh fret. Repeat this procedure on each string, working your way across the fingerboard up to the first string again. Slide your fourth finger down to tenth fret and chromatically play descending to the sixth fret. Repeat the process across the entire fingerboard. Continue until you get to the first fret and then work your way up the neck until you reach the first string, twelfth fret, fourth finger where you originally started. You can do this as many times as you wish, but for the first time of the day I recommend twice, once at a slow to moderate tempo and then again a little quicker to get the blood flowing at a faster pace.

Note that on the preceding exercise I only went to the fifth fret. If you can, go completely to the end of your neck (first fret). Remember, **NEVER** push or strain—that is when injuries occur.

Be careful to slowly build up the amount of time you practice each day. The best way to condition yourself and build stamina is to practice frequently in short sessions. No matter how much you practice, it's good to take a short break every hour. Beware of getting carried away with any one exercise or with warm-ups in general. I have known musicians who have injured themselves while stretching, which is not only counter productive, but goes against what we're trying to accomplish.

Across the Fingerboard (cont'd.)

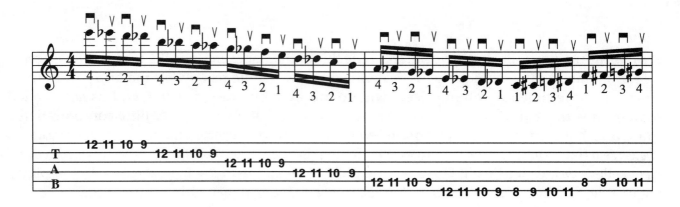

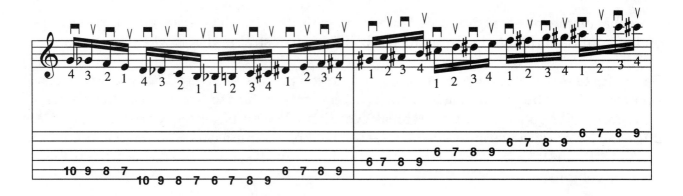

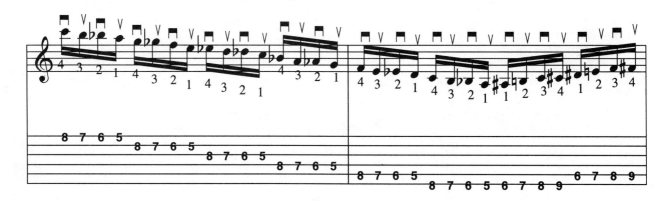

Across the Fingerboard (cont'd.)

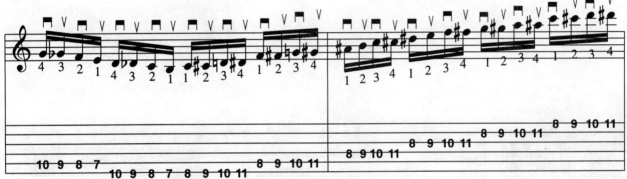

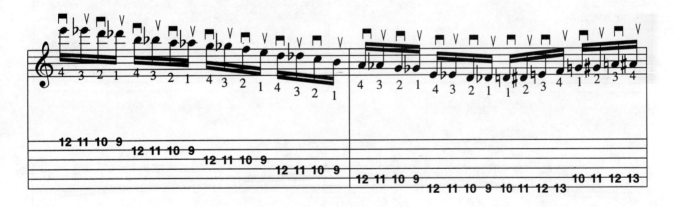

1-6 Position Switching

Switching positions has always been the guitarist's Achilles' heel. To do so in an effortless, smooth, and accurate manner is the goal for any serious guitar player. Many times we tend to spend a large part of our practice time playing positions and developing "comfort zones," leaping from one position to another instead of smoothly gliding over the fretboard. Steering away from comfort zones is an extremely difficult habit to break. This exercise not only provides an effective warm-up, but will enhance your technique and enable you to break free from the purgatory of position playing.

Move as smoothly as possible when switching positions, trying not to look at the fretboard. Only two position switches are notated on the following exercise, but once you get comfortable you can switch as many times as your instrument allows.

Practice once at a moderate tempo and then do it again at a quicker one.

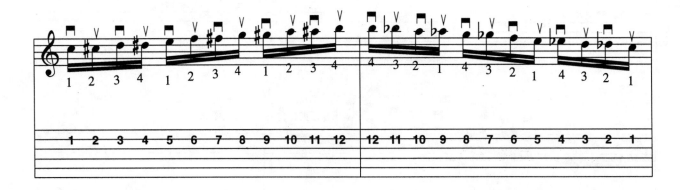

1-6 Position Switching (cont'd.)

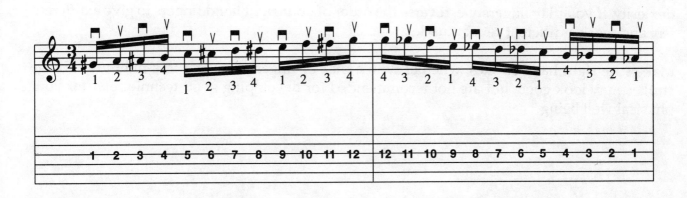

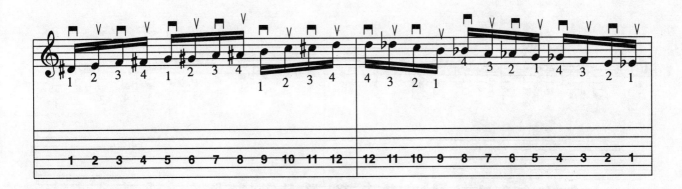

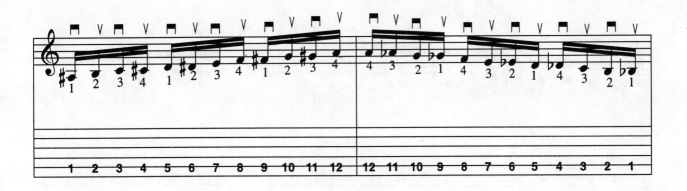

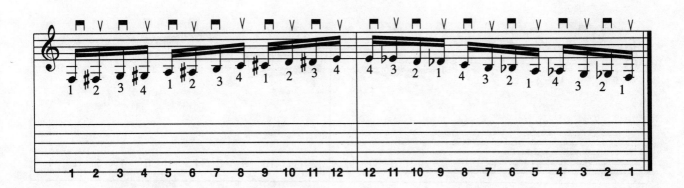

11

6-1 Position Switching

Note that on the 6-1 exercise the picking has been reversed. This will now warm-up yet another set of muscle groups. Although awkward, it is a great way to improve right hand control and dexterity. If you play fingerstyle, reverse the order of your right hand fingers to give a different feel and work a different set of muscle groups.

Make sure right hand strokes, whether with a pick or fingers, are kept to a minimum. Large strokes may look good, but are not recommended for developing good technique or for your physical well being.

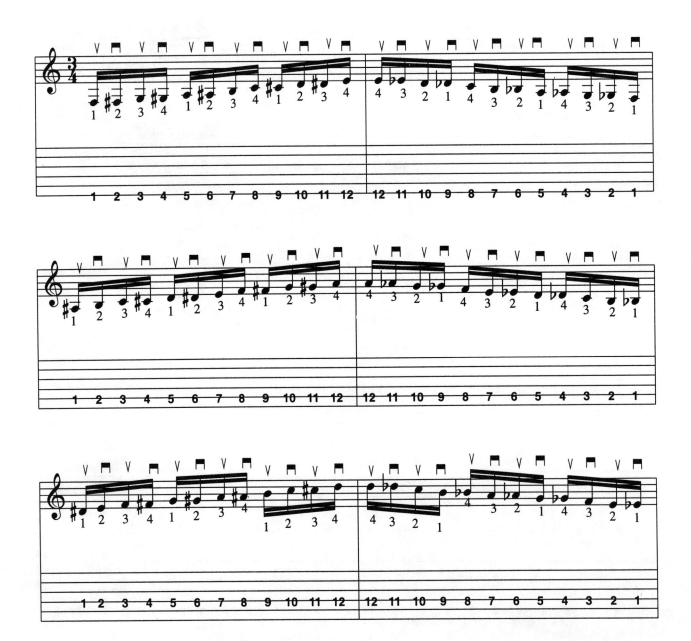

6-1 Position Switching (cont'd.)

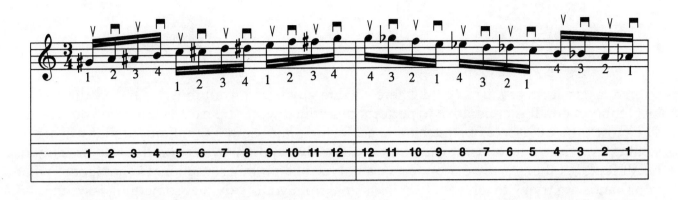

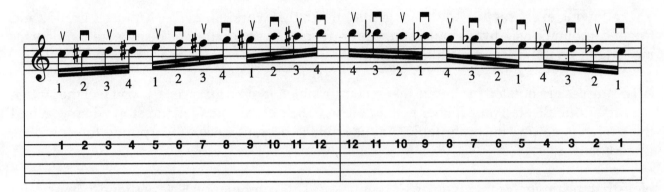

Chapter II
STRETCHES

Stretching is a form of warming up where you literally stretch your muscles and tendons—not just limber them. It is imperative to perform prescribed warm-up exercises before you stretch! The most difficult aspect of stretching is achieving a nice smooth motion without tearing or pulling muscles or tendons. It is definitely a fine line and always err on the side of caution. NEVER play if there is any discomfort or any type of a pulling sensation. Do not ignore what your hands are trying to tell you. Pain is a signal from your body that something is wrong.

The following exercises provide a nice gentle stretch that works all the basic muscle groups and finger combinations. Always make sure your fingers hover over their respective frets and never move your hand back and forth to get notes.

All examples are notated in a range that is comfortable for most guitarists. If you feel the stretch is a little difficult, start on a higher position where the frets are smaller and stop when you find the stretch is getting uncomfortable. As the stretch becomes easier, incorporate the complete fingerboard.

Note that the finger combination of 3-2 is not used. This combination is very prone to injury and you should exercise caution when using it. If all warm-ups and stretches are executed in the prescribed manner you will eventually develop a nice 3-2 stretch without having to isolate and work on it.

4-1 Finger Stretch

Place your fourth finger on the twelfth fret and stretch your first finger to the eighth fret. Move to the second string and repeat, working your way across the fingerboard until your first finger is on the sixth string, eighth fret. Slide your first finger back to the seventh fret and stretch your fourth finger to the eleventh fret. Work your way across the fingerboard until your fourth finger is on the first string, eleventh fret. Repeat this process until you reach the fifth fret. Now work your way back up the neck until your fourth finger is once again on the twelfth fret, first string.

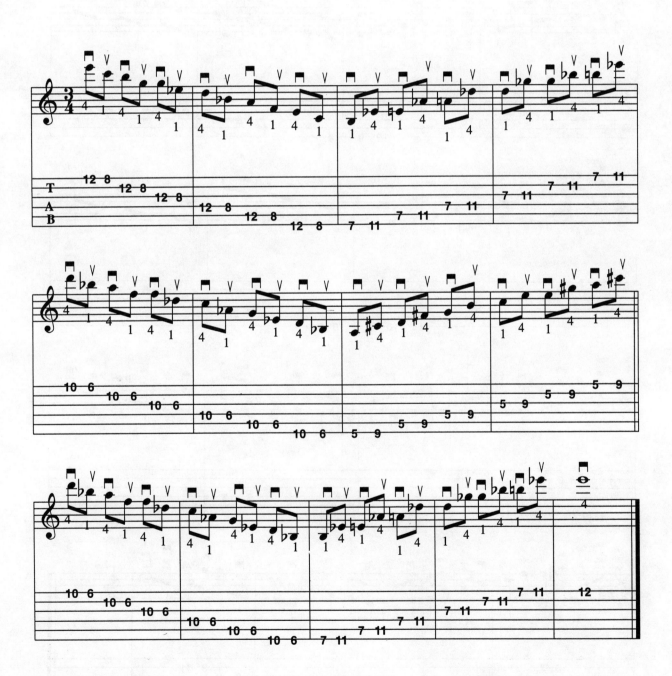

15

3-1 Finger Stretch

Place your third finger on the twelfth fret and stretch your first finger to the ninth fret. Move to the second string and repeat, working your way across the fingerboard until your first finger is on the sixth string, ninth fret. Slide your first finger back to the eighth fret and stretch your third finger to the eleventh fret. Work your way across the fingerboard until your third finger is on the first string, eleventh fret. Repeat this process until you reach the fifth fret or until it feels uncomfortable. Now work your way up the neck until your third finger is once again on the twelfth fret, first string.

2-1 Finger Stretch

Place your second finger on the twelfth fret and stretch your first finger to the tenth fret. Move to the second string and repeat, working your way across the fingerboard until your first finger is on the sixth string, tenth fret. Slide your first finger back to the ninth fret and stretch your second finger to the eleventh fret. Work your way across the fingerboard until your second finger is on the first string, eleventh fret. Repeat this process until you reach the fifth fret. Now work your way up the neck until your second finger is once again on the twelfth fret, first string.

2-1 Finger Stretch (cont'd.)

4-2 Finger Stretch

Place your fourth finger on the twelfth fret and stretch your second finger to the ninth fret. Move to the second string and repeat, working your way across the fingerboard until your second finger is on the sixth string, ninth fret. Slide your second finger back to the eighth fret and stretch your fourth finger to the eleventh fret. Work your way across the fingerboard until your fourth finger is on the first string, eleventh fret. Repeat this process until you reach the seventh fret or until it feels uncomfortable. Now work your way up the neck until your fourth finger is once again on the twelfth fret, first string. This combination is usually slightly weaker than the others, so go gently and never force any motion or stretch.

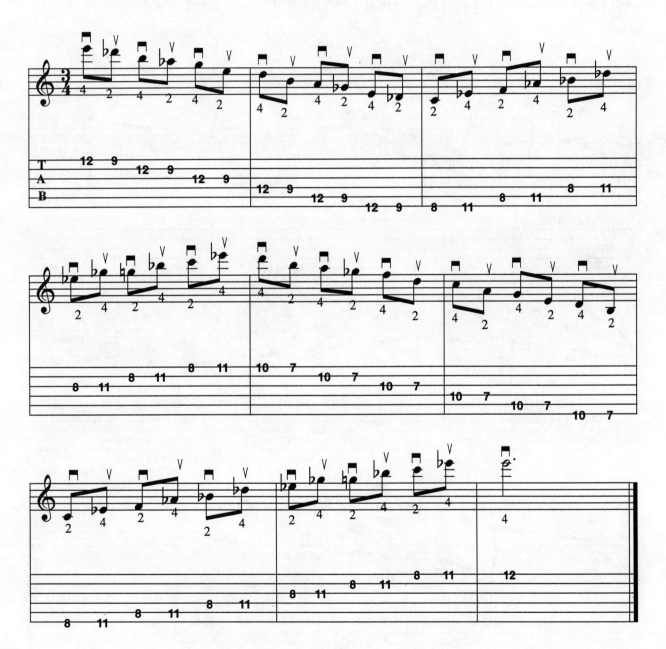

4-3 Finger Stretch

Place your fourth finger on the twelfth fret and stretch your third finger to the tenth fret. Move to the second string and repeat, working your way across the fingerboard until your third finger is on the sixth string, tenth fret. Slide your third finger back to the ninth fret and stretch your fourth finger to the eleventh fret. Work your way across the fingerboard until your fourth finger is on the first string, eleventh fret. Repeat this process until you reach the eighth fret or until it feels uncomfortable. Now work your way up the neck until your fourth finger is once again on the twelfth fret, first string. This combination is very rarely used, especially in contemporary music so you may have to start farther up on the neck where the frets are smaller to execute the stretch properly. Go slowly and the strength and flexibility will come around.

Chapter III
ALTERNATE EXERCISES

It is not necessary to make these exercises a part of your regular practice regime, but they should be used when you want to augment your warm-up and stretching routine. They not only provide a good concise workout, but also open up the fretboard in ways you may have never dreamed possible. Pick and choose the exercises you feel are the most appropriate for your physical and technical needs. These exercises are advanced, so don't get frustrated. Alternate picking is not necessary on these and you should work out a picking or right hand fingerstyle method that uses the best economy in motion for your playing style.

As in chapters I and II, never push or practice these exercises for more than a few minutes at a times; that is how injuries occur.

In Position Modal Scales

In position modal scales are a great way to get an excellent warm-up and stretch while availing many alternate fingering possibilities. The trick is to adhere to the fingering and follow the TAB so you are aware of where each note is placed. As with the other stretching exercises, make sure you are stretching appropriate fingers, not just moving your hand. After you have gone over this exercise a few times try not to look at your hands while you play and feel and listen for the proper pitches.

You will find the fingering to be, at times, extremely awkward and cumbersome, but they will provide an alternate means of playing melodies. Do not switch positions unless indicated, even though it is tempting, because that will lessen the benefits.

Once the following exercises are mastered, feel free to alter the rhythms to add variety and help develop your improvisational skills, but still adhere to the indicated fingerings. Eventually work out all the in position modal possibilities, in all keys and fingerings. The benefits will far outweigh the down time it takes to master them.

Aeolian Stretch

Latin Groove ♩= 92

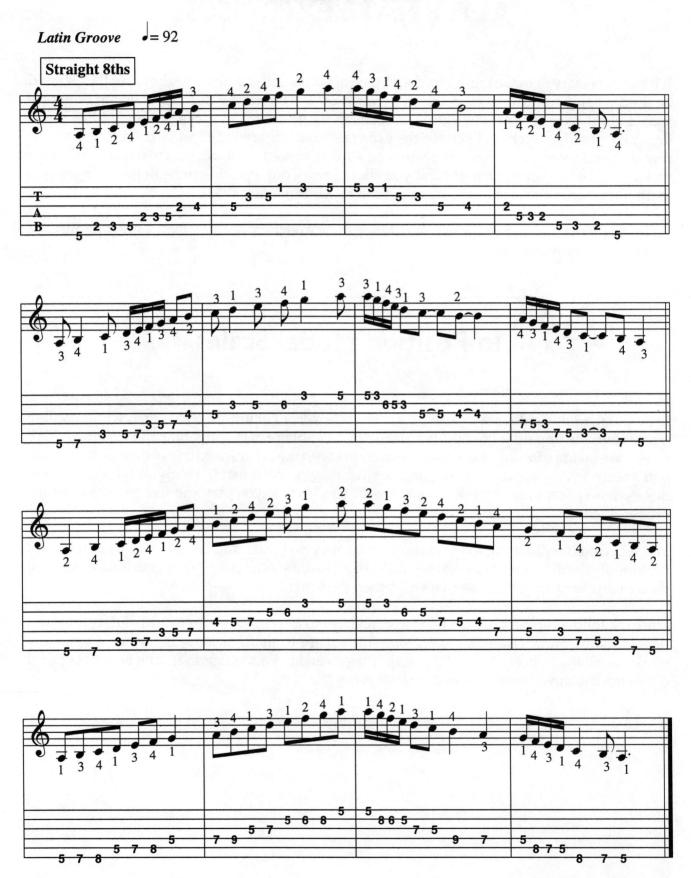

Ionian Stretch

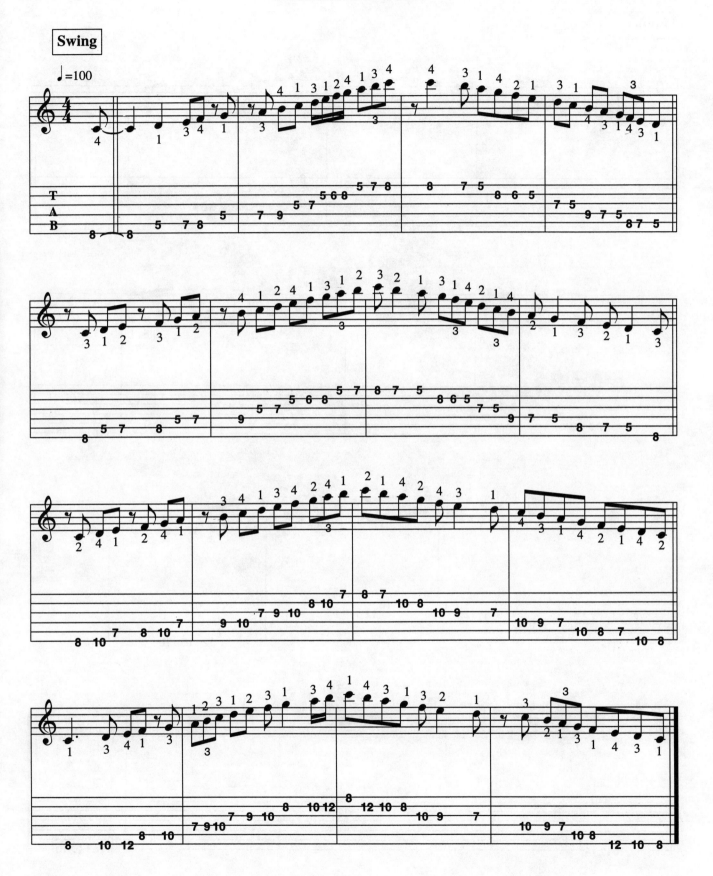

Mixo-Lydian Stretch

The Crab

The crab is a great left hand warm-up exercise that is deceivingly difficult. Make sure your fingers move simultaneously, touching the string with both fingers at the same time. This exercise is notated only through the third position, but as with the others, once you get accustomed to it, play it throughout the fingerboard.

Some say that when the exercise is executed at a medium tempo it looks like a crab is crawling up and back on your fingerboard (that is if you have a good imagination).

Fingerboard View

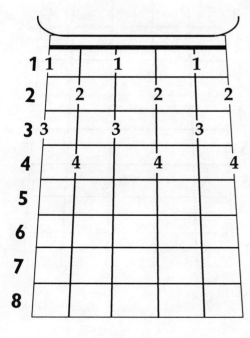

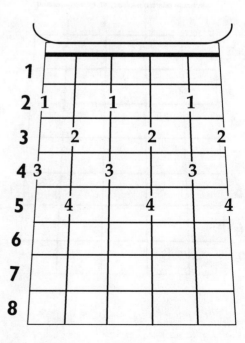

etc.

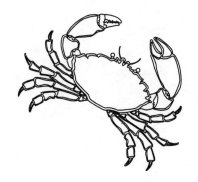
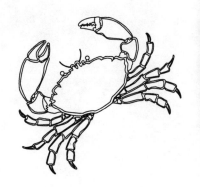

The Crab (cont'd.)

Repeat the exercise starting with fingers two and four on coinciding frets as notated below.

Fingerboard

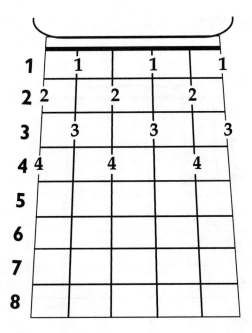
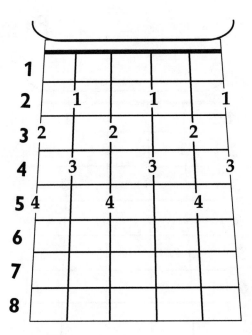

etc.

Pick and Fingers

Developing pick and finger technique has been a hit or miss situation throughout the history of guitar playing. It has been considered the bastard stepchild by both plectrum and fingerstyle players, with neither camp giving this valid technique its just desserts.

Anyone who plays with a flat pick has reached with one of their free right hand fingers to grab a note that falls at a large or awkward interval, but how many really think about what they are doing or the most efficient way of doing it? Going through the following exercises can be a very efficient warm-up with a great deal of additional benefits.

With a minimal amount of practice anyone can develop a strong pick and finger technique, taking your performance to the next level with a speed and accuracy you never felt possible.

Notation of the Right Hand

◗ = Down stroke of pick

V = Up stroke of pick

m = middle or second finger of the right hand

a = ring or third finger of the right hand

c = little or fourth finger of right hand

Pick and Fingers (cont'd.)

This is the most common combination. Note the switch on measure five; this will provide added flexibility, dexterity and overall control for your right hand.

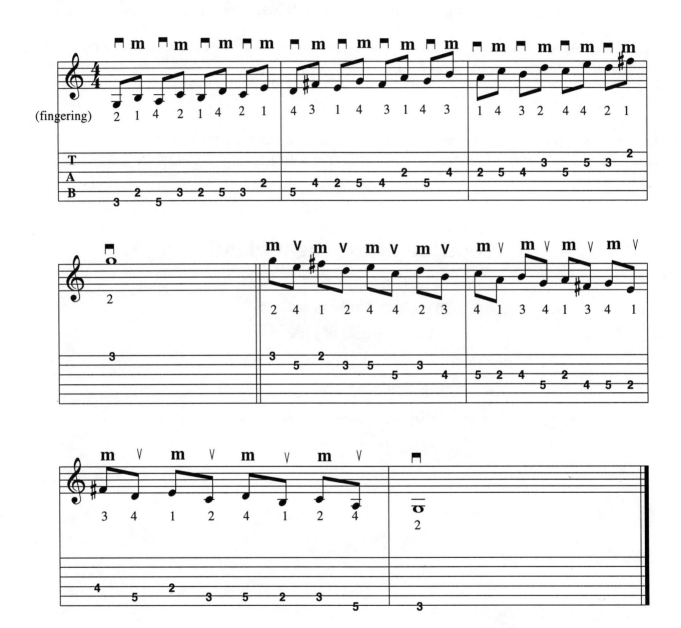

Pick and Fingers (cont'd.)

This is a little more challenging both technically and musically. It is also a much better warm-up.

Pick and Fingers (cont'd.)

Most guitarists, even classical guitarists, never use their little or fourth finger of their right hand. With a little perseverance this much maligned digit can be very useful.

Go through this warm-up (and chord example on the following page) several times daily, in short durations, and you will be surprised at how much strength and control you will be able to achieve. Your fourth finger will gradually become stronger, broadening the possibility of executing lines and chords that were never possible before.

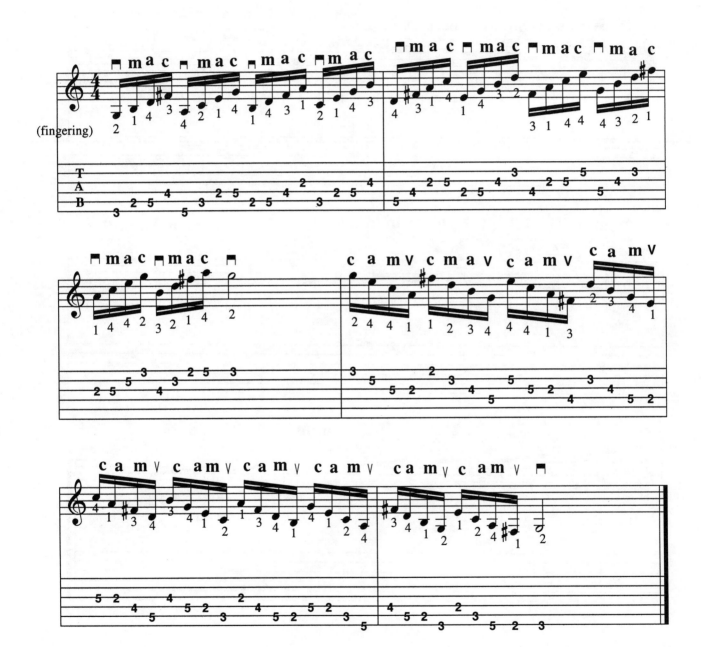

Pick and Fingers (cont'd.)
Chord Examples

Use down stroke of pick and fingers **m** and **a** on right hand for all chords.

Use down stroke of pick and fingers **m**, **a** and **c** of right hand for all chords.

The Spider Web Stretch

The following exercise will stretch the left hand and develop awesome right hand picking chops. As the "spider web" weaves its way up the guitar neck make sure you do not mute or hit strings that are not indicated.

Note the various chord extensions that appear on just about every chord. They are not marked in the chord symbols so it is a good exercise to figure out what and where they are. Many may be unusual to your ear, such as the ninth in the middle of the chord voicings on measures one and two.

Play this exercise only after you have warmed up, as it is easy to pull a muscle if you are cold. If you find the exercise too difficult, feel free to start farther up on the neck; if you are feeling limber start farther back.

Beware—this is not an exercise for those with arachnaphobia.

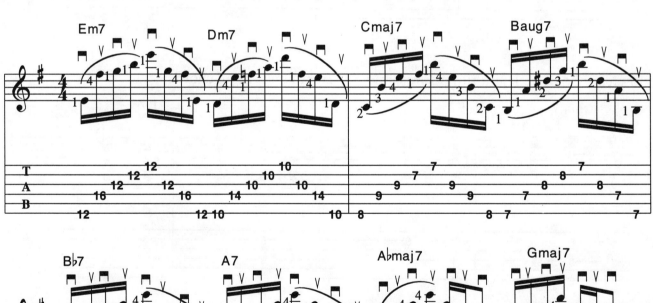